W9-AGC-374

629.227   Cooper, Jason
COO   Motorcycles

MOTORCYCLES

TRAVELING MACHINES

Jason Cooper

Rourke Enterprises, Inc.
Vero Beach, Florida 32964

© 1991 Rourke Enterprises, Inc.

All rights reserved. No part of this book
may be reproduced or utilized in any form
or by any means, electronic or mechanical
including photocopying, recording or by any
information storage and retrieval system
without permission in writing from
the publisher.

PHOTO CREDITS

© Lynn M. Stone: all photos except p. 10 © Jerry Hennen
and p. 8, courtesy of Harley-Davidson, Inc.

ACKNOWLEDGEMENTS

The author thanks the following for assistance in the preparation
of photos for this book: Pierce Harley-Davidson, Dekalb, Ill.;
Indian Motorcycle Supply, Inc., Sugar Grove, Ill.; Illinois
Kawasaki, Aurora, Ill.

LIBRARY OF CONGRESS
Library of Congress Cataloging-in-Publication Data
Cooper, Jason, 1942-
    Motorcycles / by Jason Cooper.
    p.   cm. — (Traveling machines)
    Includes index.
    Summary: Examines the history, varieties, safety aspects,
and special uses of motorcycles.
    ISBN 0-86592-494-5
    1. Motorcycles—Juvenile literature.   [1. Motorcycles.]
I. Title.   II. Series: Cooper, Jason, 1942-   Traveling machines.
TL440. 15.C66   1991
629.227'5—dc20   90-26928
                                            CIP
Printed in the USA   AC

TABLE OF CONTENTS

Motorcycles   5

Parts of a Motorcycle   6

The First Motorcycles   9

Modern Motorcycles   11

Dirt Bikes   14

Street Bikes   16

Special Motorcycles   19

Motorcycle Safety   20

The Wonder of Motorcycles   22

Glossary   23

Index   24

MOTORCYCLES

Vroooom! Everyone knows the roar of a motorcycle. Motorcycle engines have big voices. Still, motorcycles are the smallest motor vehicles that can travel on highways with cars and trucks. Even the largest motorcycles weigh only about 900 pounds, far less than a small car.

Like bicycles, motorcycles usually have two wheels. But a motorcycle has wider tires, a heavier, more rugged steel **frame,** and a gasoline-powered engine. The engine is midway between the motorcycle's wheels. The engine allows a motorcycle to travel as fast—or faster—than a car.

Modern motorcycle

PARTS OF A MOTORCYCLE

Motorcycles have handlebars, just as bicycles do. A motorcycle rider, or **biker,** controls speed by turning the **throttle** on a handle grip. A biker has one hand brake and a foot brake.

The handlebars are mounted on two steel tubes called **forks.** The motorcycle's forks keep the front wheel in place. The forks are attached to the motorcycle frame.

Some of the other parts of a motorcycle are rear view mirrors, exhaust pipe, windshield, and **kickstand.**

Motorcycle controls

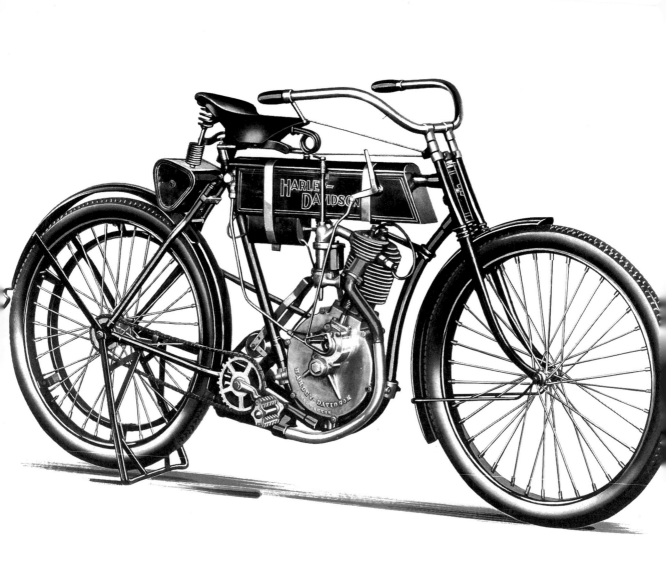

THE FIRST MOTORCYCLES

In 1885, Gottlieb Daimler attached a motor to a wooden bicycle frame in Germany. The first motorcycle was born!

For several years, other inventors experimented with frames and motors. By 1897 a truly useful motorcycle had been built in France. When World War I began in 1914, the motorcycle proved itself. It took over many jobs once performed by horses.

After the war ended in 1918, motorcycles became popular as quick, cheap transportation.

1903 Harley-Davidson motorcycle

MODERN MOTORCYCLES

The motorcycle's looks have not changed much. Modern motorcycles have kept the shape of early "bikes," as motorcycles are often called.

Modern motorcycles, however, are far more powerful and easier to handle than their ancestors. They are also more comfortable and more likely to run well.

Today, Japanese companies sell over half of the world's motorcycles. The only American motorcycle builder is Harley-Davidson in Milwaukee, Wisconsin. Indian, a popular American brand for about 50 years, went out of business in 1953.

1991 Harley-Davidson motorcycle

Last of the Indians, 1953 model

Fixing up a 1941 Indian motorcycle

DIRT BIKES

Most motorcycles are built to be used on either dirt tracks or paved roads. Off-road bikes, or dirt bikes, are lighter than the motorcycles that operate on streets.

Off-road bikes weigh between 100 and 225 pounds. They have narrower tires and rougher treads than street motorcycles. Many dirt bikes are used for racing at speeds up to 80 miles per hour.

Kawasaki "dirt bike"

STREET BIKES

Street bikes are the motorcycles built for paved roads. They range in size from about 250 to 900 pounds. The biggest of these are touring bikes, which easily handle two riders.

Touring bikes can be used for long-distance travel. They have many comforts, like a backrest, radio, and cruise control.

Several kinds of bikes are streamlined with plastic **fairing** sections. The fairing helps reduce wind force.

A few street bikes can reach nearly 200 miles per hour.

Kawasaki "street bike"

SPECIAL MOTORCYCLES

Some motorcycles are built for special purposes. A two-purpose motorcycle, for example, can be used on and off city streets.

Motorcycles with side cars have three wheels. The side car is not a real car but an open carrier used to hold luggage or another person.

Choppers are motorcycles with extra-long front forks and small front tires. Many of the original parts of choppers have been cut, or chopped, away.

Minicycles are small lightweight motorcycles.

Motorcycle for on- and off-road use

MOTORCYCLE SAFETY

Motorcycle riding can be dangerous as well as fun. Motorcycle riders on highways travel at the same high speeds as automobiles. Motorcycles, however, are much smaller than cars, and their riders have little protection.

Motorcycle riders are offered a class by the Motorcycle Safety Foundation. In the classes, people learn how to ride safely and avoid problems with other vehicles.

To protect themselves, many bikers wear helmets, **goggles,** leather jackets, and boots.

Helmets and leather for safety

THE WONDER OF MOTORCYCLES

Motorcycles give their riders a sense of freedom. For street bikers, the open highway calls. Dirt bikers are lured by the **Motocross** and **Enduro,** two of the American Motorcyclist Association's best-known events.

People once owned motorcycles because they needed low cost transportation. Now bikers own motorcycles because they want to. What better way to taste the wind than to roar off on rolling wheels?

Glossary

biker (BI kur) — a motorcyclist; one who rides a motorcycle

chopper (CHAH pur) — a motorcycle changed by its owner; a motorcycle with unusually long forks

Enduro (en DUR o) — motorcycle racing over long distances in open, wooded, and hilly country

fairing (FAIR ing) — a plastic structure added to motorcycles to reduce wind effects

forks (FORKS) — steel tubes in front of a motorcycle that support handlebars and keep the front wheel in place

frame (FRAME) — a structure; a motorcycle's body before tires and trim

goggles (GAH guhls) — protective glasses

Motocross (MOTO kross) — motorcycle racing on an off-road track

kickstand (KIK stand) — a metal rod used for keeping a two-wheel vehicle standing upright

throttle (THRAH tul) — a device that determines a motorcycle's speed by controlling the flow of gasoline

INDEX

American Motorcyclist
  Association   22
biker   6, 22
car   5, 20
chopper   19
Daimler, Gottlieb   9
dirt bike   14
Enduro   22
engine   5
fairing   16
forks   6, 19
frame   5, 6
France   9
Germany   9
handlebar   6
Harley-Davidson   9, 11

Indian   12, 13
Motocross   22
Motorcycle Safety Foundation   20
racing   14
safety   20
side car   19
speed   14, 16
sound   5, 22
street bikes   16
throttle   6
touring bikes   16
truck   5
weight   5, 16
wheels   5, 6, 22
World War I   9